NAVMC 2645

THE MANAGEMENT SURVEY

I0426422

U.S. MARINE CORPS

PCN 100 013326 00

DEPARTMENT OF THE NAVY
HEADQUARTERS UNITED STATES MARINE CORPS
WASHINGTON, D. C. 20380

ABA/WRC/hlm
17 May 1972

FOREWORD

1. **Purpose**

   This publication, NAVMC 2645, THE MANAGEMENT SURVEY, is a guide for conducting management analyses at all echelons of command and staff. Consequently, a wide variety of methods and techniques are provided in a flexible organization so that individual users can adjust these general procedures to fit their own needs. Specifically, the purposes of this publication are:

   a. To acquaint commanders and supervisors with the need for, and benefits of, a management survey.

   b. To serve as a guide to the management engineer or analyst in conducting a management survey.

2. **Requisitioning Instructions**

   See MCO P5600.31A, Publications and Printing Regulations.

3. **Certification**

   Reviewed and approved this date.

   ORMOND R. SIMPSON
   Lieutenant General, U.S. Marine Corps
   Deputy Chief of Staff (Manpower)

DISTRIBUTION: A plus 7000 less 7000080
              plus 7000080 (50)

PCN 100 013326 00

THE MANAGEMENT SURVEY

RECORD OF CHANGES

Log completed change action as indicated.

Change Number	Date of Change	Date Received	Date Entered	Signature of Person Entering Changes

THE MANAGEMENT SURVEY

Contents

THE MANAGEMENT SURVEY

Chapter 1

AN OVERVIEW OF THE MANAGEMENT SURVEY

1001. Introduction

a. To the commander or supervisor, the Management Survey is a service designed to determine potential managerial problems and to highlight opportunities to eliminate waste or unnecessary use of resources.

b. To the management engineer or analyst, it is a tool used to evaluate how well an organization is performing its functions in the accomplishment of its mission and how efficiently the available resources of manpower, money, material, and facilities are being used to that end.

c. Based upon a well-executed management survey, managers can institute or modify policies or procedures to enhance the economical effectiveness of their organizations.

1002. Areas Reviewed by a Management Survey. The management survey reviews all operations of the organization and makes appropriate recommendations. It examines, with a view toward improvement, such areas as:

a. Mission. Is it in agreement with that of the next senior echelon? Is it being accomplished? Is it in writing and clearly understood by all members of the organization?

b. Functions. Are they necessary for mission accomplishment? Are they actually being performed, as defined in writing, and specifically assigned?

c. Organization. Is it logical and clear? Is it understood by the employees? Is the span of control reasonable?

d. Methods and Procedures. Can they be improved, simplified, combined, or eliminated? Would mechanization effect an improvement? Are standing operating procedures used whenever practicable? Has a procedures manual been prepared and kept current?

e. Personnel Requirement. Is there a realistic relationship between work volume, job difficulty and manpower?

f. <u>Personnel Utilization</u>. When a task is assigned, is commensurate authority needed to perform the task also delegated?

g. <u>Quality and Quantity of Work</u>. What type of review is conducted to insure acceptable quality? Are there too many reviews? Have realistic quality and quantity standards been determined and are they being met?

h. <u>Reports</u>. Are unnecessary or duplicate reports required or prepared by the organization? Are reporting instructions for required reports clear and concise and do they call for only necessary information? Do they provide all the necessary information to do the job?

i. <u>Forms</u>. Are forms being used to the maximum extent possible to reduce typing volume and preparation time and to insure standard format? Is there unnecessary duplication among forms? Are forms designed to facilitate completion?

j. <u>Records</u>. Are inactive records, which are no longer required by the organization, disposed of properly and in accordance with current instructions? Are file cabinets being used for files and not for storage? Are records maintained in an orderly arrangement to provide rapid filing and retrieval?

k. <u>Office Equipment</u>. Is equipment on hand being utilized efficiently? Is it the proper machine for the job? Can a savings be effected by substituting a machine for manual effort? Are surplus office machines and supplies returned to the supply officer for reissue to other activities?

l. <u>Working Conditions</u>. Is the office layout designed to provide personnel with maximum available space? Are personnel who have frequent contacts situated near each other? Does the layout permit a straight line flow of work? Does it take full advantage of natural light? Are aisles of the proper width?

m. <u>Correspondence Practices</u>. Are preprinted form letters used whenever practicable? Are correspondence shortcuts in use by typists? Are pattern paragraphs and letters used to the maximum extent when letters must be manually prepared? Would automatic typewriters be economical?

The foregoing listing may be expanded during the course of the survey depending upon conditions uncovered. In some surveys, it will not be necessary to review all of the areas listed. Also, at times, specialized surveys are conducted placing emphasis in one area, e.g., personnel utilization, methods and procedures, or office equipment. Chapter 4 outlines some of the factors to be examined in various specialized surveys.

1003. **Who Conducts A Management Survey?** The Marine Corps has many sources of expert managerial assistance to conduct surveys. Management offices staffed with management analysts and/or industrial engineers exist at most major commands. Since a complete survey involves a thorough review and analysis of every aspect of an organization, it requires a team of qualified specialists who must spend considerable time exploring the mission and functions, the organizational structure, the efficiency of methods in use, utilization of the work force, productivity, cost of operation, and many related aspects. There are several advantages to such professional surveys:

a. The management analysts are selected for their ability to perform such studies on the basis of their training and experience.

b. The management analysts can devote full time to the survey without distraction and without neglecting other work.

c. The management analysts are an impartial group. They have no axe to grind; their only obligation is to perform a complete and objective study, arrive at sound conclusions, and make workable recommendations that will benefit the organization and the Marine Corps.

d. The management analysts, being an outside group, are not concerned with day-to-day operations, and are in a position to take a fresh look at the organization's systems, policies, and practices.

No matter how much knowledge management analysts bring with them, management surveys must be cooperative ventures. Operating personnel must contribute their knowledge and experience. The more technical the work of the organization, and/or the more involved the operating problem, the more dependent will the management analyst be on operating officials to obtain facts and interpretations on which to base recommendations. It is essential that there be full understanding, mutual respect, confidence and cooperation between the management analyst and the operating personnel.

THE MANAGEMENT SURVEY

The commander of the organization being surveyed, upon
the request of the management analyst, should assign a competent member of his staff to work with the analysts. The staff
member will furnish technical and background knowledge to
assist in solving problems, and his participation in the study
will provide him with training in the application of management survey principles. Inclusion of an operating official on
the survey team may increase the confidence of other operating
personnel and facilitate acceptance of recommendations. Additionally, the commander must make it clear to all his subordinates that he favors the survey. There is no substitute for
command interest. If favorable results are to be obtained,
and savings are duly affected, he must give public assurance
to the management analysts that they have his full support and
he must direct his subordinates to extend complete cooperation.
The commander should make himself available to discuss problems
and propose solutions during the course of the survey. When
necessary, he must reassure his subordinates if they become
apprehensive as a result of the survey. He must resolve
differences of opinion upon survey recommendations. Finally,
it is imperative that he take positive action to see that
accepted recommendations are installed as soon as practicable
and are given a fair chance to work.

1004. Where Should A Management Survey Be Conducted? A management survey may be conducted in any organization or in any
element of an organization in the Marine Corps. A management
survey may be performed for any one of several reasons. Some
of these are:

a. Internal management problems -- within a command such
problems as an increased backlog, failure to meet deadlines,
and decrease in personnel performance may dictate the need
for a management survey.

b. Imposition of external controls -- controls imposed
by higher authority, such as lower personnel ceilings or
fund limitations, may require a survey to find ways of coping
with the new conditions.

c. Establishment of a new organizational component --
when a new activity is being organized, the management analysts
can frequently contribute valuable assistance in establishing
an organization structure and in formulating effective,
economical procedures.

d. Determination of the need for a survey by the organization commander -- the commanding officer of the activity,
the officer in charge, or the supervisor of a subordinate
unit may recognize weaknesses in operations and request a
management survey to correct unfavorable conditions.

e. Establishment of a management survey program -- when a program of recurring management surveys is established at stated time intervals, management analysts conduct a survey of each organizational component. After a thorough basic study, succeeding studies may be comparatively brief audits unless conditions have changed sufficiently for another detailed management survey. The recurring management survey, or management audit as it is sometimes called, seeks to ascertain whether the organization is performing its mission satisfactorily on a continuing basis.

1005. What Type of Savings Can Be Realized After the Management Survey? Implementation of the recommendation of the management survey can result in increased efficiency and economy in the use of men, money and material. Improved methods, better means of control, more efficient operations and greater use of human and physical facilities will lead to the elimination of waste and inefficiency.

1006. Summary. This chapter has defined the management survey, given reasons for its undertaking and listed typical areas that may be analyzed by this means. The advantages of having a survey conducted by trained analysts or engineers have been cited. The need for strong support by the commander for the survey has been justified. Savings will most likely be realized by the implementation of survey recommendations.

Chapter 2

PREPARING FOR THE MANAGEMENT SURVEY

2001. Surveys Must Be Systematic. A management survey is a systematic examination of an organization and its functions. The management analysts review and analyze the structure, functions and procedures in use in order to identify problems, find the causes and recommend solutions. A systematic approach must be emphasized. Unless a predetermined plan is followed, the results of the management survey are likely to be incomplete or inadequate. Without a plan, the survey may drag and become unnecessarily costly in terms of time spent by the analysts and operating personnel. A predetermined plan is necessary in order to avoid confusion and wasted effort. A systematic examination aids the analyst in collecting and interpreting data, in arriving at sound conclusions and in presenting recommendations for adoption. This does not mean that the management survey plan, once made, cannot be changed. It should never be so formalized and inflexible that it cannot be altered to meet special circumstances or changes in conditions. The survey plan is a guide which will help the management analyst to make a systematic and comprehensive study of the organization without wasting time and effort, and to develop recommendations that will improve operations.

2002. The Survey Request. The request of an organization for a management survey should be in writing, and should be addressed to the management support activity and be signed by the head of the organization requesting the survey. The request should be brief but specific. It should identify that which the organization believes to be the basic problem.

2003. The Initial Interview. After receiving the request for a survey, the management assistance office will normally assign an analyst to interview the head of the organization. Occasionally, it may be necessary to discuss the proposed survey with an officer higher in the chain of command, but under any circumstances, it is imperative that the management analyst reach a firm understanding regarding the survey with the immediate head of the activity being studied. During the initial interview, the management analyst should obtain a brief history of the organization and any other data which are readily available, such as organizational charts of the activity, organization manuals, and statements of mission and functions. The analyst should ask the activity head to discuss as many problem areas as he is able to identify, explain their origin and state what is being done to solve them. During the preliminary interview, the management analyst should discuss the contribution expected of the activity during the survey. The activity head should be requested to assign a competent subordinate to work with the analyst and should agree to make himself available to discuss problems and proposed solutions. The management analyst should inform the activity commander of the steps to be taken preliminary to the actual survey, such as the explanation of the survey to employees, the giving of job security assurances to subordinates, and requests for cooperation. These steps will be discussed in subsequent paragraphs.

2004. <u>Orientation of the Employees</u>. Employees of the organization should be informed of the management survey as soon as agreement to conduct it has been reached. Prompt notification will do much to prevent false rumors and ungrounded fears. A memorandum distributed to each employee is perhaps the best way to announce the survey. The memorandum should state the reason for the survey and that a management analyst or team of analysts has been requested to make the survey in an effort to improve organization and procedures. It should state clearly that the activity head supports the aims of the analyst and urge cooperation by all employees. It should further state that the management analysts are authorized to deal directly with supervisors to arrange interviews and that the supervisors are to furnish the analysts with any information they may request.

2005. <u>The First Group Interview</u>. Following the announcement that a survey is to be made, an initial group interview should be held. Civilian employees should be given as much assurance of job security as can be offered. Steps of the survey should be explained to the employees and an opportunity to ask questions should be afforded them. They should be informed that there will be a reconnaissance survey to develop the management survey plan, and they should be briefly informed of the various fact-finding techniques which may be used during the survey. They should be assured that any recommendations for change in organization or operations developed during the survey will be fully discussed with the activity head before acceptance or implementation. Every effort should be made to enlist employee participation in the survey. It should be made clear to all supervisors and workers that suggestions and recommendations are welcomed and will receive consideration. Appropriate recognition should be granted to employees whose suggestions are adopted.

2006. <u>Assurance to Employees</u>. It is essential that the civilian employees be given as much assurance of job security as is feasible. At the out set of the survey, employees may be fearful of losing their jobs, of lower prestige, and of reduced income. Unless such fear is dispelled, it is difficult to obtain full cooperation; employees are likely to react defensively in replying to questions and may exhibit a resistance to change. Under these conditions, the survey will lose some of its effectiveness. The assurances given to the employees must at all times be honest. If a survey is aimed at making personnel reductions, it is futile to assure them that there will be no loss of billets. However, assurances can be made that wherever possible, normal rather than forced attrition will be utilized to accomplish the required reduction, and that the activity personnel officer will help any employee to find a new job if he should be displaced as a result of survey recommendations. Whenever the survey is being conducted to improve organization and methods, this fact should be emphasized along with any benefits which employees might receive from the survey.

2007. <u>The Reconnaissance Survey</u>

a. Following the interview with the head of the organization and the orientation of employees, the management analysts will normally perform a reconnaissance survey. A reconnaissance survey is a preliminary examination of the organization. It is used to determine, in a general way, the scope of the problem and the best course of action to follow. The length of the reconnaissance survey varies and in some instances it is dismissed entirely, depending upon the familiarity of the management analyst with the organization. During the reconnaissance survey, the analysts should gather the facts that they will need to formulate the survey plan. They should determine whether the problem areas which they discover during the reconnaissance survey can best be solved by a management survey or whether a less expensive method can be used. If they decide that a management survey is justified, they will define its scope and ascertain whether the problems arise within the organization or are caused by elements beyond the control of the organization, thereby possibly extending the area of the survey.

b. During the reconnaissance survey, the management analysts may conduct brief, selective interviews with personnel in order to obtain a general impression as to the level of morale, the volumes and kind of work, and the type of skill and knowledge possessed by employees. They will make general tours through the activity and observe procedures and working conditions. They will be especially interested in discovering the nature, size and age of the backlogs which may exist. The analysts will examine administrative reports of the activity and note the trend and volume of work and of manpower requirements. If the reports indicate excessive labor turnover, the causes will have to be identified during the survey and corrected if possible. The growth or decrease in responsibilities within the organization may indicate the trend which planning for the future should take.

    c. Following the reconnaissance survey, the management analysts will summarize their findings and discuss their preliminary conclusions with the officer who requested the survey. If the problem of the activity can be solved by a less expensive course of action than a management survey, the requesting officer will be so informed at this time. If, on the other hand, the management survey should be conducted, the management analysts will be prepared to discuss with the authorizing officer and/or the immediate head of the activity the following:

    (1) The nature and extent of the reconnaissance survey.

    (2) The findings of the reconnaissance survey.

    (3) The objectives of the management survey to be conducted.

    (4) The number of analysts who will conduct the survey.

    (5) The beginning date of the management survey and the approximate time it will take.

    (6) The assignment to the survey team of an individual to represent the organization.

    d. The foregoing may be oral or written. Much of the information will be contained in the survey plan.

2008. <u>The Survey Plan</u>. Immediately following the discussion with the officer requesting the survey, a survey plan is prepared. The plan is a point of departure for the survey, and replanning is conducted as necessary during its course. The survey plan should be comprehensive and contain sufficient detail to become a plan of action, but the management analysts must avoid establishing an inflexible schedule which might be made unworkable by unforeseen circumstances. Appendix A is an example of a management survey plan.

2009. <u>Summary</u>. A management survey should be conducted systematically and follow a predetermined plan. This plan must be flexible to meet changing conditions during the survey. Upon receipt of the written request for a survey, the management engineers should interview the activity head to obtain background information. As soon as a survey has been decided upon, the employees should be officially informed and their groundless fears dispelled. The management team should seek the cooperation and participation in the survey of all supervisors and employees. During the reconnaissance survey, the analysts should gather the facts they will need to formulate the survey plan; this they do through interviews, a general tour, and an examination of the work. They make a report of the reconnaissance findings to the authorizing officer and/or to the immediate head of the activity. Finally, they prepare the survey plan, which will serve as the operating outline for the management survey.

Chapter 3

FACT FINDING

3001. <u>Simplifying Work</u>. Most of the procedures followed in clerical and administrative work can be simplified. Management analysts conducting a survey at any command frequently will uncover duplicate records, excessively detailed reports, useless statistical compilations and handy-dandy information collected just in case someone should ask for it. Such records, reports and statistics become voluminous if left unchecked. These innocent-appearing papers steal man-hours from productive work, waste money and material needed for carrying out primary responsibilities, and use valuable floor space required for accomplishing the activity's mission. Much progress is still needed to replace obsolete procedures, reduce excessive recordkeeping and eliminate useless tasks.

3002. <u>General Principles in Fact Finding</u>

a. While following the survey plan as closely as possible, management analysts should not permit the plan to restrict their search for pertinent facts. They should be constantly alert to the possibility of attaining additional data which will be beneficial to the survey. They should at all times maintain flexibility as to where and how to gather facts. It should be noted that few phases of a survey can be exhaustively treated within the time and resources allotted. Analysts must be wary of the temptation to exceed the limits of the survey and the time schedule set forth in the survey plan. It is more important to give the commanding officer a timely, workable solution when he expects it than to postpone the report for several weeks in hope of developing a cure for all problems.

b. The management analysts should determine the types of facts they will require for diagnosing and solving the management problems. They should determine how they will use the facts they gather. It is useless to spend hours accumulating data concerning procedures that cannot be changed because of legal or other restrictions. The fact-finding phase should follow the management survey plan as closely as is practicable. If major deviations from the survey plan become necessary, the plan should be amended to reflect the new conditions. It is better to gather too many facts then too few. The facts, figures and forms should be organized systematically by subject in accordance with the survey plan. In gathering data, the management analysts will do well to first procure all of the facts and figures available from easily accessible sources, such as administrative reports, organizational charts, functional lists, correspondence, procedures manual, position descriptions, working papers, records, laws, regulations, inspection reports, and budget estimates. This information will provide valuable background material and its analysis may lead to a requirement for additional information concerning the activity. The analysts should use those methods of fact finding which will provide accurate data with the least disruption of the work of the activity.

3003. Fact-Finding Methods

    a. There are four commonly used ways to gather facts during a survey:

        (1) Study the existing records.

        (2) Questionnaires.

        (3) Interviews.

        (4) Personal observations.

    b. The procurement of information by studying various records pertaining to the activity has already been discussed.

3004. The Questionnaire. The questionnaire has special use in management survey work. It can be used to obtain information when there is insufficient time to interview all of the people from whom the information is wanted. Interviewing a sampling of the personnel may be preferable to the use of the questionniare, however. The questionnaire is a useful technique when the management analysts wish to obtain concise information that can be tabulated readily. It can be used as a device for obtaining information from personnel on detached duty. It has the advantage of allowing the person completing the questionnaire sufficient time to perform any necessary research. However, the questionnaire has some limitations. Many people feel that it is an overworked device and will not respond to them. It is sometimes difficult to phrase questions with such clarity that misinterpretation will not result. Questionnaires are impersonal. The management analysts have no contact with the person furnishing the data and are unable to form impressions as to their qualifications to provide accurate information. If a questionnaire is used it should be brief, clearly stated, free from ambiguity, and answerable by one word or a short statement. The questionnaire should be so phrased that the answers can be tabulated and conclusions drawn from the data. It is important that the questionnaire be distributed only to persons who are able to provide accurate information, that the personnel receiving the questionnaire understand its purpose and that they be informed that it has the full support of the commander. If the questionnaire is to receive wide distribution, it should be tested on a small group to make certain that the questions are clear. Random samplings may be useful in selecting the group upon which to test the questionnaire. Every effort should be made to obtain a 100% reply since those who do not answer may be persons whose replies are particularly significant.

3005. The Interview

a. The interview is a basic fact-finding technique in management surveys. It is virtually impossible to conduct an effective survey without employing interviews to some extent. It is a prime method for securing information recorded only in the mind of the person being interviewed. Frequently, an employee can suggest a method for simplifying his work, but is reluctant to discuss it with his supervisor. The interview is a useful means of encouraging employees to formulate and present their suggestions. During the interview, the analysts look for all facts relative to the organization procedures being studied. Additionally, the analysts cross-check to make sure the information gathered is correct. The interview permits observant management analysts to gather information in addition to what is told to them. An interview with a supervisor gives the analyst an opportunity to evaluate the supervisor's attitude, knowledge and qualifications. An interview with a worker is the best way to judge how well he is trained, his morale and whether instructions and policies are clear to him. The management analysts can also use the interview to impress upon the workers the need for their cooperation in furnishing facts and ideas, if maximum benefits are to be obtained from the survey. The analysts can dispel the erroneous impression that there is something mysterious about management analyses, and that problems can be solved by drawing answers out of thin air without the hard work of gathering and evaluating the facts. The following rules for interviewing may prove helpful:

4003. An Approach To Solving A Survey Problem. The paragraphs
which follow relate a problem-solving process to the types of
problems that analysts are likely to meet in the management
survey. This procedure does not guarantee that the management
team will arrive at the right answer every time. It is
intended to help management personnel use a systematic approach
to problem solving and to avoid making snap decisions based
on intuition.

a. The management analysts should identify specific
unsatisfactory conditions -- things that are wrong; e.g.,
the work is delayed, it costs too much to accomplish, or it
contains too many errors. When they have stated the problem
clearly, they are well on their way to solving it.

b. The management analysts should relate the unsatisfactory conditions to underlying causes. This goes hand-in-
hand with problem identification. Sometimes, while seeking
to learn what causes a problem, they find that they have
merely identified the symptoms, not the problem itself. For
example, the problem may appear to be that the work is delayed.
Is this the problem, or just a manifestation of a high rate of
sick leave? Why the excessive sick leave -- is it due to
falling office morale? What causes the low morale -- is it
due to poor supervision? Perhaps the real problem is how
to get better training for supervisors. The management analysts
cannot learn the basic difficulty until they have analyzed the
situation. They begin with a known factor -- a knowledge of
an unsatisfactory condition. They identify as many potential
factors as possible; those they ascertain to be implausible,
they discard; those which they cannot explain but which appear
to be pertinent, they study further; those which are obviously
relevant, they trace back to their sources. In effect, they
separate the problem into its various parts to assist them
in identifying the underlying causes. When they have determined the causes for the problem, their course of action may
become apparent.

c. The management analysts should explore the interrelationships of the unsatisfactory conditions, e.g., determine
whether a large backlog is causing errors in the other work
being produced. They should group those difficulties which
arise from identical causes. By correcting a few basic sources
of unsatisfactory conditions, they may be able to eliminate
many management problems.

(1) Explain to each person you interview what information you want and what you are going to do with it.

(2) Listen, don't talk; encourage the worker to talk.

(3) Do not criticize nor make hasty suggestions. Be friendly and courteous - let the worker know you are genuinely interested in his work.

(4) Use simple language, trying to pick up terminology having special meaning to the employee.

(5) Avoid conversational detours - they are time wasters.

(6) Take detailed notes as you go along - it is impossible to remember all of the facts in most interviews.

(7) Tell him you may return even if you later find it to be unnecessary.

b. The management analyst should use care in selecting personnel to be interviewed. He should arrange a logical sequence of interviews which will provide him with the maximum amount of information. Interviews should be on an individual rather than a group basis. In scheduling interviews, the management analysts should remember the time requirement of the individual worker to complete urgent jobs for which he is responsible. Prior to the interview, the analyst should devise a number of questions, the answers to which will produce the kind of information the analyst wants. The analyst should avoid time wasting conversation on detours which contribute nothing to the survey. However, the interview should be as informal as possible. While recording the procedures and other information obtained during the interview, it is helpful to have copies of the documents being discussed. Supervisors and workers should be requested to bring with them to the interview a completed copy of each document, record, report, form and sample of correspondence with which they work. These will increase the analysts' understanding of the process, and will usually facilitate fact finding.

c. While the interview is an invaluable fact gathering technique, it contains limiting factors which must be considered. Personnel being interviewed are frequently asked to

provide information which they have not had an opportunity
to verify. They may guess at some of the answers to give
information which is only approximately correct. Other
individuals unconsciously try to answer questions the way
they think the management personnel would like them answered,
even if they have to depart from the facts. Sometimes the
worker subsequently denies statements he has made during an
interview and the analysts may meet resistance to the interview itself. Impatience of the worker to get the interview
over with so that he can get back to his job, reluctance
to discuss work difficulties because of the worker's fear
of being disloyal, and complaints which have no bearing on
the problem at hand are some of the problems which will
hinder the successful accomplishment of the interview. Some
individuals tend to build up areas of autonomy around which
they erect fences barring an analytical approach by the
management analysts. Some personnel are fearful that as
a result of the interviews, pet procedures will be changed
or personal power diminished.

3007. Personal Observation

a. The fourth fact-finding method, personal observation,
is extremely important. Personal examination is the only
positive method of verifying the facts given in reports,
records, questionnaires and interviews. First hand observation will clarify hazy impressions and will provide the
management analysts with the information they need to overcome groundless resistance to change. It assists the survey
staff to become better acquainted with the supervisors and
employees. Observations of the operation prove invaluable
to management analysts when they are assisting in the installation of procedures they have recommended.

b. There are several observation techniques. The type of
information sought and the source from which it can be obtained
will determine the technique to be used. Frequently, it is
desirable to verify doubtful information by checking it at
different operating points or by using different techniques.
A general tour, as outlined in the reconnaissance survey, will
identify symptoms of administrative disorder and the analysts
may attempt to determine the causes and to find cures for
these disorders. Tracing procedures is another useful technique. During the interview, the management analyst identifies
certain procedures and methods followed by the activity. A
careful record should be made of each procedure, and the forms,

reports, records and correspondence related to that procedure should be kept with it. In tracing procedures, it is important to distinguish between a record and an action form. The record form is merely a history, while an action form requires someone to do something. The analyst's survey will not be complete until information is obtained on all of the basic documents. Desk audits are used to verify material furnished to the management analysts during interviews. Audits are of particular value in determining individual responsibilities, details of workflow, personal knowledge and attitudes, and effectiveness of a training program. The management analysts must be certain that the desk they select for audit is representative of the activity. A review of incoming and outgoing correspondence may tell the management analyst a great deal regarding how effectively the organization accomplishes its mission and how long it takes to process requests for information. It may provide background information which will give the analyst a better understanding of the operation. Such a study will help to evaluate the methods used to prepare correspondence, which is frequently an area of large potential savings when preprinted forms, letters, pattern paragraphs and automatic typewriters can be substituted for manually typed letters prepared from rough drafts, long hand notes or dictation.

    c. Since the volume of work to be accomplished is normally a major determinant of paperwork flow, production statistics should be studied whenever they are available. Additionally, backlogs should be carefully investigated. A backlog indicates an area requiring remedial action, and a growing backlog adversely affects administrative processes, particularly when personnel are subject to criticism despite their best efforts to keep the work current. The management analysts will render the activity a service when they can devise ways of eliminating backlogs. This can frequently be accomplished by improving and simplifying the procedures, by using mechanized processes, by replacing manually prepared letters with preprinted forms, by eliminating unessential recordkeeping, and by reducing reviews to a minimum. Whenever there is a backlog of any size, control should be installed to insure that the oldest and the most important transactions receive priority attention. In some organizations, backlogs are seasonal due to peakloads and will normally be reduced over a period of time. In other instances, backlogs are acceptable when required actions do not have to be completed in a specified time frame and the number of required actions remains fairly constant.

d. The management analysts should carefully examine the files of the activity, since the files are an excellent means of acquiring an understanding of the operations and how well they are being conducted. The analysts will be interested in what type of material is being filed, whether the proper filing system is being used, and whether inactive or obsolete material is being retired or destroyed in accordance with regulations. Any unofficial records retained by the organization should be carefully scrutinized to see whether they are necessary. Unofficial records come into being when the workers are unable to obtain the data they need from the official files. These should be carefully examined with a view toward expanding the official files if the additional information is deemed necessary for performing the work and eliminating all unofficial records. The following questions are useful in examining records and files:

(1) Do the office records duplicate files retained elsewhere in the command?

(2) Can desired information be secured by telephone instead of duplicating another file?

(3) How often are the files and records retained in the office consulted?

(4) Do office personnel trust their records or do they verify the information before using it?

(5) Does the office keep files simply because it always has done so?

(6) Are all copies made utilized?

(7) Is the information contained sufficiently useful to justify retention of each record?

e. The working environment should be examined critically to see what effect it has upon production. Insufficient space, poor lighting and high noise level generate inefficiency. Often, insufficient attention is paid to the proper arrangement of an office to insure that work will flow from desk to desk instead of requiring personnel to move. The analysts should review the office layout at the completion of the survey and recommend changes which will improve working conditions, permit a straight-line flow of work, facilitate supervision and promote accessibility.

3007. General Rules in Surveying

a. The following general rules in surveying should prove helpful to the management analysts:

(1) Without accurate and complete data, recommendations may be merely educated opinions. There is no room for guess work in analysis, and solutions must be based on facts. Recommendations should never be influenced by favoritisms, prejudice or value judgments. When the management analyst has obtained facts accurately and completely, the solutions to problems will frequently be self-evident.

(2) Few people like to be the subject of a management survey. It is imperative, particularly during the fact-finding phase, that the management analysts carefully weigh every word and action to avoid criticizing unjustly or inaccurately.

(3) Any survey will create some disturbance. Interference with operations and actions which may be injurious to morale should be kept to a minimum. This can best be accomplished by tact, open-mindedness and a constructive approach.

(4) Never suggest changes for the sake of change. If management analysts are unable to improve an operation, they should avoid discussing it in the report. Nothing is gained by writing a study report on a procedure they cannot improve.

(5) Always weigh the cost of making a change against the savings which may be effected by the change. If the purchase of an $8,000 machine can be expected to make a long range savings of only $3,000, buying the machine is a waste of money. If, on the other hand, an annual savings of $3,000 can reasonably be expected, the purchase should receive full consideration.

(6) It is not always easy to get personnel to stand still for a time-consuming, thorough survey. There is often heavy pressure for immediate action, and a recommendation that lengthy study and analyses should come first frequently provokes impatience. The more intense the pressure for immediate change in a complex situation, the greater the likelihood that the

analysts will overemphasize symptoms and ignore underlying causes. Pressure for prompt action may be barrier to adequate diagnosis.

(7) Management analysts should project themselves into the position of a responsible employee and decide whether they would be willing to work under conditions created by their recommendations. This is particularly true when they are recommending a reduction in personnel. They should be convinced beyond any reasonable doubt that the personnel complement they are recommending will be a sufficient force.

(8) Beware of the exception when an interviewee is illustrating a point by citing an example. The management analysts should determine whether he is discussing an interesting but exceptional case or a recurring action of the type with which the analysts are concerned.

b. For some management surveys, the use of charts may be helpful. Charts can have great value in presenting a large mass of data in condensed form without sacrificing essential details. They are a means which permits management analysts to visualize the entire series of operations in a way not possible by the use of other methods. Charting clarifies methods and procedures, and facilitates analysis. Appendix B provides instructions for the preparation and analysis of the more commonly used charts in a management survey. Other charts such as statistical, pictographic, curvilinear, bar logarithmic and PERT charts may also be useful to the management analysts educated in their construction and interpretation.

c. Checklists are a tool to help the management analysts cover every facet of an organization during the survey. The questions on the checklist are designed to facilitate analysis. The answers should result from study and review of the facts, with a view towards correcting management weaknesses and accomplishing savings in manpower, money and material. The checklist which is appended as appendix C is suggestive, not exhaustive. The management analysts should add to it from their own background and experience in accordance with the requirements of the survey.

3008. Summary. The management analysts conducting a management survey are likely to meet resistance to change based on the traditional way in which an operation has been performed. When something has been done in a particular way for many years, it is probable that it can be done more easily and cheaply. Most procedures followed in clerical and adminis- trative work can be simplified. Surveys should be contained within the limits of the problem and the time schedule, unless specific authority to exceed the plan has been granted. It is better to collect too many facts than too few, and these must be organized for ready availability. Systematic fact finding is essential to an effective survey; the management analysts must determine the types of facts they will require for diagnosing and solving the management problems and devote their efforts to collecting these types of facts, making such changes in their survey plan as are necessary because of new or unforeseen conditions. There are four major fact-finding methods used in a management survey. These are: the study of existing records; the questionnaire; interviews; and personal observation. Finally, this chapter lists eight general rules to be considered in conducting a management survey.

Chapter 4

ANALYZING THE FACTS

4001. <u>Fact Finding and Analysis Occur Simultaneously</u>. As
the management analysts gather facts during a survey, they
concurrently analyze them and form tentative conclusions.
These analyses assist them in their fact finding, either by
indicating that additional information is needed, or by making
it evident that no significant improvement is possible and there
is no point in spending further effort to obtain additional
data. There is no clean, sharp line between survey and analysis.
Fact gathering, analyses and formulation of corrective procedures sometimes blend together. The management analysts accu-
mulate a formidable array of material; procedures statements,
organizational charts, functional statements, tables of
organization, statistical data, office layouts, lists of
equipment, interview records, and voluminous notes during
their survey. As they have proceeded to collect this data,
they have also conducted some analyses and formulated some
tentative conclusions. The material gathered should now be
organized for further analysis.

4002. <u>Analysis and Synthesis</u>. Analysis and synthesis are the
basis techniques for improving any organization, procedure,
policy or practice. In improving an organization, the management analysts arrange the facts, so as to determine their
interrelationships and their bearing on the problem. They
must ascertain what is done, why it is done, who does it,
where it is done, when it is done, and how it is done. They
must examine each individual step in the process and decide
whether it can be done better, or perhaps in a different
way, no matter how efficient the present system may appear.
Analysis is the separation of anything into its elements.
It is an examination to distinguish the component parts of
the whole, separately, in relation to each other. The purpose of an analysis is to prepare for synthesis. Synthesis
is the combining of separate parts or elements so as to form
a whole. It is opposite of analysis. By analysis and synthesis, an organization, a procedure or an idea is broken
down into its elements and then recombined into a new or
different form to produce and improve a more effective plan.
In some instances, the data collected will lead the analysts
to an obvious conclusion. In other situations, there will be
multiple variables which are complex.

d. The management analysts should <u>develop alternative</u> ways of dealing with unsatisfactory conditions. This is the step in the problem-solving process which calls for creative thinking. The job of the management analysts is to list as many possible solutions as they can visualize. They must keep an open mind and write down every possible solution that occurs to them, the plausible and the implausible. Evaluations will come later. The more possible solutions they can develop, the greater their chances become of eventually arriving at the best solution, instead of merely one that may work but has several flaws. Research may reveal how other activities have overcome similar problems. The management analysts should continue to study the various factors of the problem as long as they can develop additional solutions and explanations. Their job will be easier if they can eliminate their preconceived notions and keep open minds to such questions as "how else can it be done;" "what else is causing the problem;" "where else is it being accomplished;" and "when else could it be done better?" When they have run out of ideas, they can sometimes profit by reviewing the problem and then laying it aside to work on something else. This will get them out of the mental rut in which they have been concentrating, and give their subconscious minds a chance to incubate the problem. When they return later, they may find a fresh insight has helped them to develop additional possible solutions.

e. The management analysts should <u>select one solution</u> from the alternative ways of solving the problem. Here they must exercise judgment -- the most important attribute of a management analyst. They should compare the advantages and disadvantages of the various methods of dealing with the problem. When the obviously impracticable plans have been eliminated, and the remaining ones have been matched against the administrative goal to be attained, e.g., more accuracy or fewer manhours to accomplish the work, a few possible solutions may look promising. Frequently, the best solution will be a combination of two or more of the possible solutions in that it brings together the strong points of each and eliminates glaring weaknesses. The more hard work, skill and imagination the management analysts employ in this phase of the problem-solving process, the better the chances of developing a solution that is not only adequate, but the best possible under the existing circumstances.

f. The management analysts should <u>test the proposed solution</u> before installing it. They will do well to seek the opinions of the people directly involved in the work -- supervisors, technicians, and senior clerks. From them the management team may be able to obtain expert opinion on both the feasibility and the weaknesses of the proposal. It is at this point in the problem-solving process that the proposed solution is carefully scrutinized and tested to make certain that it contains no hidden weaknesses which would create problems rather than solving them.

g.   The management analysts are now ready to implement the solution to the problem. The plan that looked so good on paper and even worked well in a pilot study may develop weaknesses in actual practice. Accordingly, when they imple- ment the solution, they should watch the results carefully. First, they work out and follow an implementation schedule, to include indoctrinating key personnel, giving assistance where needed in making changes, and taking corrective action wherever necessary. The management analysts should partici- pate fully in making the changeover to the new plan and recognize their responsibility for successful installation. If the problem disappears when the new plan has been install- ed, the management personnel know they have developed the right solution. If it does not disappear even after adjust- ments have been made to meet unforeseen circumstances, they should work their way back through the problem-solving process. They should review the other possible solutions to see whether one of these would have worked better, or whether they might have overlooked a pertinent fact that would have given them a different viewpoint on the whole problem. If there is still no solution, the management analysts should make sure they have correctly defined the problem they have been trying to solve. It may be that despite all their work, they arrive at the wrong solu- tion because they had been trying to solve the wrong problem. In any event, if the new plan works, they should give due credit to the supervisors and their assistants. If the proposal, after a fair trial, is unsuccessful, the analysts must bear the major part of the blame.

h.   The management analysts should follow-up each solution they implement. After the new plan has been in operation long enough to evaluate its effectiveness, the management team should check with the head of the organization to ascertain whether maximum results are being obtained. Refinements of the plan can now be worked out and installed to completely elimi- nate the unsatisfactory condition the management analysts were initially called upon to solve.

i.   There are many pitfalls which analysts may encounter while conducting a survey or audit. The most common reason for survey failure is faulty planning within the survey staff. Appendix D lists the common mistakes made by analysts in surveys. With proper planning the analysts will normally avoid the pitfalls noted. Additionally, the analysts are cautioned that the rules and procedures set forth in this chapter cannot be utilized in isolation while conducting an analysis. The analysts must be thoroughly familiar with all of the procedures and their relationship to one another. There is no easy way to conduct a survey, and thoroughness is a prime essential. Surveys involve human beings who may not be subjected to precise solutions that may be indicated in statistical tables or by theoretical principles of management and organization. The basic, obvious rule which is often violated is that the efforts of the analysts should be directed at the solution of problems and not the pursuit of certain techniques. There is no one best way to conduct an analysis; the analysis staff must be flexible in its plan, methods and approach.

4004. Summary. During the fact-finding phase of the survey, the management engineers are concurrently analyzing the facts they have gathered. Facts must be organized before they can be successfully analyzed. Analysis is the separating of anything into its component parts; synthesis is the recombining of the parts into a new whole. Analysis and synthesis are basic to effecting an improved plan, procedure, or organization. In analyzing a problem, the management analysts should identify specific unsatisfactory conditions, relate them to underlying causes, explore the interrelationships of the unsatisfactory conditions, develop alternative ways of dealing with them, select one solution to the problem, test the proposed solution, install it in the activity, and subsequently follow-up to see that their plan is working satisfactorily.

Chapter 5

DEVELOPING, PRESENTING, AND IMPLEMENTING RECOMMENDATIONS

5001. <u>Basic Missions of A Survey Team</u>. The management analysts on a survey team have three missions: to identify the problem, to solve the problem, and to obtain approval of, and implement the solutions. These solutions are the recommendations for improvement. Good recommendations are of no value unless they are adopted; poor recommendations adopted as a result of superior salesmanship may prove harmful. Good recommendations must be developed and put into effect if the survey is to be successful.

5002. <u>Developing Recommendations</u>

a. A broad approach to the problem should be used in developing recommendations. Examine the problem in relation to the entire organization or organizational entity. Measure the problem against known standards of good management.

b. The purpose and scope of the study have an important bearing on the organization of the facts. The general rule is to group the facts according to the objectives of the survey, any external factors that should be resolved, and the major steps of the proposed system. Under any method of organizing the facts, the survey should be broken down into digestible portions, treating the most significant points first.

c. Many problems can be solved by an analysis of the organization. This analysis may reveal that functions can be eliminated, consolidated, expanded or established. One primary principle in systems problem solving is to look for eliminations. An entire function may be eliminated if it does not contribute to the objective or costs more than the benefits derived. Each operation must contribute more than it costs.

d. The solution must fulfill the objectives of the survey. As the facts are analyzed, logical methods occur to the analyst and he attempts to relate the details to the true objective of the system. The details have been questioned as to necessity, objective, place, time and personnel to perform the work. Another consideration should be the availability of resources to implement recommended solutions. Management analysts must not concentrate on streamlining the performance of present systems when they should be visualizing and conceptualizing the final results.

e. Established policies enter into every systems development. The management analyst must determine if management will change the policy. In many instances, policy is established by higher authority or by another government agency. Management analysts should contact the "policy makers" during the study phase to determine what positive actions can be recommended as regards future changes in policy.

f. The proposed recommendations must completely satisfy the problem as it is defined in the study. They may be more comprehensive than the original problem required. When the proposed system represents a comprehensive change from the existing system, with significant investment in new equipment and installation cost, a detailed comparison of the costs of the two systems is required. It may be necessary to know clerical time and cost factors. When a pilot study cannot be made, the analysts must resort to more ingenious methods of determining clerical standards and costs. Many times, it may be necessary for the analysts to roll up their sleeves and perform all processing functions to determine work standards and costs.

5003. Presenting Recommendations

a. After the management analysts have gathered, reviewed, and analyzed the facts and developed recommendations, they are ready to present their findings. This is usually done by a survey report.

b. The report of survey serves several purposes. It is an instrument for:

(1) Providing the organization surveyed with a formal document to use in carrying out the recommendations.

(2) Furnishing a summary of the findings and conclusions of the management analysts.

(3) Informing the activity commander of the recommendations that have been accepted and put into effect by the organization being surveyed.

(4) Obtaining the decision of the activity commander on recommendations not accepted by the organization surveyed, but which the management analysts continue to support.

(5) Providing the management office or agency with a document for aiding in the installation of recommended procedures, if required.

c. The presentation of systems recommendations and reports is usually done in writing, and procedures are written to make the systems known to all persons of the activity required to read the report - the commander, supervisors and operating personnel. The supervisors and operating personnel must understand the report, for they will be required to implement it. The success or failure of the management analyst's work may often hinge on the effectiveness of the survey report. Reports which concisely and graphically present the important points in easily understood language will have the most appeal. The nature of the assignment and the type of study dictate the type and extensiveness of the report.

d. Types of Survey Reports. There are three types of survey reports. These are:

(1) Installation Reports - sometimes used where recommendations are installed during the course of the survey; the report merely reports on the action taken.

(2) Letter-type Reports - when the scope of the survey is limited to a short study involving usually one specific problem.

(3) Formal Written Reports - most reports of management surveys are of this type.

e. Preparing the Survey Report. There are many variations in arrangement and content of a survey reports, depending on the subject and scope of the investigation, the length of the reports, and the audience for which the report is written. The report should be packaged in an attractive manner. Below are listed some elements that are required in every report; some are optional:

(1) Letter of Transmittal. A letter of transmittal is the usual method of forwarding the survey report. This letter may be brief (it may give only highlights of the recommendations) or it may list all recommendations.

necessary for accomplishment of the mission. It is possible that several persons may perform various tasks necessary to carry out a specific function. Each task reported on the Task Lists must be related to a specific function. After the Task Lists are received, the Work Count or Volume should be completed on the Function List.

    b. <u>Preparation of the Work Distribution Chart</u>. The Work Distribution Chart is prepared from the data collected on the Function List and the Task Lists. This Chart presents the work performed in the organization under current operating procedures. A sample Work Distribution Chart appears as Tab C. The chart should be prepared in the following manner:

    (1) Functions contained in the Function List should be shown in the first column. List the functions from top to bottom in the order of relative importance in terms of time required for performance. Leave space between the functions.

    (2) Individuals should be listed by name, grade and billet title from left to right in order of responsibility. Begin listing with supervisor and continue down to the lowest grade.

    (3) Tasks, as originally listed on the Task List, should be listed in the person's column opposite the functions to which they are related.

    (4) Hours spent by each person on each task are recorded in the "Hours Per Week" column opposite the tasks. Hours are totaled for each function and recorded in the "Hours Per Week" column for the function. The total hours worked per week are recorded on the bottom of the page and are determined by totaling the hours for each function.

    (5) Work count data from the Task Lists are entered under the proper column for each task. Work count data for each task are totaled and entered under the proper work count for the function.

    c. <u>Analysis of Work Distribution Chart</u>

    (1) After all of the function and task data have been recorded the Work Distribution Chart is ready for study and

(2) <u>Cover or Title Page</u>. The title or subject of the study should be completely descriptive but concise. It should include a project number if assigned. The <u>names</u> of the analysts participating in the survey are normally listed on the cover or title page; the project officer of the survey should also be shown. The <u>date</u> the survey report is submitted should be shown on the title page when the report is not submitted by a transmittal letter.

(3) <u>Tables of Contents</u>. The various parts of the report, illustrations and special features should be listed, showing page numbers for easy reference.

(4) <u>Introduction</u>. The introduction is usually divided into the following segments:

(a) <u>Origin and Authority</u>. This segment should include a statement of the origin of the investigation - who requested it, when it was requested and what was requested.

(b) <u>Purpose and Scope</u>. The purpose and scope of the survey requested should be stated in full. If the survey required going beyond the scope requested, this fact should be stated and justified.

(c) <u>Acknowledgments</u>. Acknowledgments of cooperation, assistance and contributions received from various personnel should be included. Acknowledgments should be generous but not flowery.

(5) <u>Summary</u>. The summary should be brief so that the commander, who may not have the time to read the entire report, may gain an overall picture of the investigation. A brief resume of the salient points covered in the discussion section should be included, as well as a short statement of the conclusions and recommendations.

(6) <u>Definitions</u>. In some cases, several of the terms used in the report may be subject to various interpretations. If this is the case, a section defining these terms should be included in the report.

(7) <u>Discussion</u>

(a) This is the analytical section and the principal part of the report. It presents the facts disclosed by the investigations and the recommended solutions. An historical presentation of past occurrences is valuable as background for the current analysis. A section of the report may be devoted to detailed presentation and analysis of the proposed alternatives which appear most desirable. Alternate recommendations are usually submitted when a large investment in equipment is required to implement a new system. Alternate solutions may also be necessary when the newly proposed system may encompass the entire organization and the phases of implementation may need to be staggered. Sometimes the analysts may come up with three solutions, all workable. When this is the case the recommendations should be listed in the order of preference, giving the advantages and disadvantages of each alternative system.

(b) The discussion section should include the mission and function of the activity being studied; the organization, including the organization or organizational functional chart; the staffing and manpower utilization, including proposed table of organization listing the billet description, present grade, proposed grade if applicable, and the number of personnel for each billet discription and the procedures.

(c) The procedural section should be organized in a logical and readily understandable fashion. A number of different logical approaches are usually possible. The analyst must examine all possibilities to provide the simplest and clearest organization of the material. Procedural material is usually most effective when presented in chronological sequence; that is, the activities of the organization are explained in the sequence in which procedures are performed. Then the personnel concerned with certain functions need only read the procedure applicable to them. Procedures should not refer to personal names but should use organizational titles.

(8) Appendix. The appendix of the report should contain statistical tabulations, exhibits, charts, visual aids and written instructions for the installation of the proposed system, blueprints and other data which do not properly fit into the body of the discussion. A list of references and persons supplying various parts of the information may be included in a lengthy survey. When it is attached, the list of references should be constructed in a standard bibliographic format.

5004. Implementation of New Systems and Procedures

a. Although it is the responsibility of the line organization to install the actual procedures, the analysts must stand ready to assist in the installation of a plan by supplying advice as required.

b. It is desirable that those concerned with carrying out the new procedures participate in their development. When one takes part in formulation of a plan, he feels responsible for making it work. On the other hand, resistance to change is a fundamental attitude present in all people in varying degrees. The best of plans has been known to fail because those principally engaged in carrying it out were not consulted in its development and, as a result, had made up their minds before testing that the changes would not work. Consulting with all concerned prior to the installation stage is important to successful installation.

5005. Putting the Recommendations into Effect

a. Putting recommendations into effect is the joint responsibility of the line and staff organizations, with the planning and coordination being done by the staff analyst. The analyst cooperates closely with supervisors throughout installation.

b. Without actually taking over the responsibilities of the various changes, the analyst should constantly audit the performance of supervisors in the area of personnel relations. The attitudes of personnel are important to the success of the new methods. Also, adequate plans must be made for personnel transfers, reductions and training.

c. As he works with the supervisor in getting ready for the installation, the analyst should be able to develop numerous work aids and office workplace rearrangements that will aid in the operation of the new system. In this preparatory work, unforeseen problems requiring solution are likely to develop, and some minor modifications of the proposed system could be required. All these details should be handled as promptly as possible and management advised of progress being made toward installation.

d. The final timing of the actual changeover is important. Whenever possible, it should coincide with slack periods of the year or month, or some logical conversion period. It must be recognized that a new system requires a certain period of time in which to develop the efficiency expected of it. Additional, temporary help may be required during the pilot run or breaking-in period. It is better to use temporary help where possible than to require excessive overtime on the part of the regular personnel. If unforeseen delays make the planned starting date unrealistic, it is wise to delay the start rather than jeopardize the success of the installation. Care must be taken that replaced functions and duties are actually discontinued at the time of the changeover, or as soon as feasible.

e. Neurschel provides ten rules for making a major changeover that bear repeating:[1]

(1) Be ready before starting.

(2) Keep up to schedule.

(3) Avoid rash, emergency decisions.

(4) Anticipate and eliminate crises.

(5) Don't let minor kinks dampen your enthusiasm or your confidence in the plan.

(6) Keep all phases of the changeover coordinated by informing executives and supervisors promptly of any changes in the original procedures of the installation plan.

(7) Prevent dissension among the personnel.

(8) Don't require continuous or excessive overtime work of the installation crew. If the changeover is falling significantly behind schedule because of lack of personnel, get some extra temporary help.

(9) Avoid disruption of service.

(10) Don't sacrifice thoroughness for speed.

---

[1]R. F. Neurschel, "STREAMLINING BUSINESS PROCEDURES" (New York: McGraw-Hill Book Company, Inc., 1970), p. 262.

5006. Follow-up

a. After installation, the methods job is not complete until there has been a follow-up by the systems analyst. This follow-up has several purposes:

(1) Determine that objectives of the system are being accomplished. Are anticipated cost savings being realized? Is the quality of the information resulting from the system in accordance with the planned standards? Are time schedules being maintained and is output of the system on schedule?

(2) Determine that all parts of the new system are actually operating. Sometimes minor phases of the system are left unstarted in favor of concentration on the major parts of the system.

(3) Make whatever modifications or refinements in the system and written procedures as may be justified by actual operating experience.

(4) Make sure that all replaced routines are actually discontinued.

b. Subsequent review of the system is desirable at infrequent intervals. However, proper cooperation with the internal audit staff should satisfy this requirement.

5007. Summary

a. The survey report is also useful to the organization in carrying out the recommendations. It furnishes a summary of the findings and conclusions; it informs the commander as to which recommendations have been adopted and effected; it is a means for getting decisions on disputed recommendations; and it provides the management engineering office with a document for follow-up. The three types of survey reports are installation, letter-type and formal written reports.

b. It is better to institute improvements by convincing all concerned, rather than by forcing adoption by order of the commander. Resistance to some of the recommendations can be expected.

APPENDIX A

EXAMPLE PLAN FOR A MANAGEMENT SURVEY

Plan for a Management Survey of the Disbursing Office

1. <u>Purpose</u>. To assist the Disbursing Officer to accomplish his workload with a reduced personnel strength.

2. <u>Scope</u>. To cover all phases of administration in the Disbursing Office.

3. <u>Management Analysts Assigned to Survey</u>:

Major W. R. Campbell, Jr., Management Engineering Branch
Mr. J. B. Stewart, Management Engineering Branch
Major W. G. Reddick, Disbursing Officer

4. <u>Major Problems (as revealed by Reconnaissance Survey)</u>:

a. Workload exceeds capability of staff to accomplish during regular working hours, requiring much overtime.

b. Excessive number of errors in enlisted accounts.

c. Large turnover of civilian clerks.

d. Excessive recordkeeping.

5. <u>Major Steps of Survey and Tentative Time Table</u>:

a. Review of regulations and directives: 7 - 11 April

b. Fact finding: 14 April - 9 May

To be accomplished by personal interviews and observations, and review of correspondence and reports:

(1) Organization and functions
(2) Staffing and personnel practices
(3) Methods and procedures
(4) Reviews and audits
(5) Records and files
(6) Work standards
(7) Reports and forms
(8) Equipment
(9) Layout

6. <u>Analysis of Facts and Preparation of Recommendations</u>:

 12--23 May

7. <u>Preparation of Final Report and Preparation of Recommenda-
tions</u>:

 26 May--6 June

8. <u>Installation of Approved Changes</u>: 9--27 June

 (Recommendations for minor improvements are frequently
 adopted and installed during the fact-finding and analysis phases. This paragraph refers to more complex
 changes which may not be completely installed during
 that time.)

9. <u>Follow-Up Survey</u>: To commence 15 December

APPENDIX B

ANALYSIS BY CHARTING

1. Depending upon the type of organization a management analyst is called on to survey, charts may be very helpful in his analysis. The more commonly used charts within a survey are the Work Distribution Chart and Flow Process Chart.

2. The Work Distribution Chart (DD 1724)

    a. Preliminary Requirements. The Work Distribution Chart is prepared from data collected on the Task List and the Function List, two locally reproduceable forms. Examples of these lists appear at Tab A and Tab B to this appendix.

        (1) Preparation of the Task List. The Task List should be prepared by each person in the organization being surveyed. Each will fill out the first six blocks at the top of the form and then describe in their own words, specifically, each task they perform. For example, don't say "type forms." Name the form such as "type public works requisitions" or "type weekly muster reports." Each task will be identified by a number starting at one and appearing under the column titled "Task Number." After each task is identified average the number of hours spent on each task per week and record on the form. Recurring tasks such as monthly or quarterly reports should be prorated and recorded on a weekly basis. For example, a task done once a month requiring eight hours is recorded as two hours per week. The last entry, per task, is the work count. Enter under the appropriate column the number of times each task is performed per week.

        (2) Review of Task List. After the Task Lists are collected and reviewed, they should be discussed in detail with the person who made out the list. It is important that the analyst understand each and every task listed in order to develop a comprehensive Work Distribution Chart. Do not change the contents of an individual's Task List without first conferring with the individual.

        (3) Preparation of the Function List. The Function List is prepared by the analyst. The first five blocks are completed. List and number each function that the organization performs. The performance of these functions is

analysis. It must be remembered that the chart is a method for arranging facts concerning the division of work in a clear and understandable manner. It provides a basis for systematic questioning, but does not necessarily offer ready answers to these questions. The answers are a product of study and analysis, together with the experience and common sense of the analyst. Therefore, while studying the Work Distribution Chart of the existing organization, notes should be made on this chart. Since it is extremely important to know what to look for, the following questions should be asked about each item on the chart:

(a) What Functions Take the Most Time? Are these the functions which should take the most time? Normally, the largest total time should be devoted to the major function of the organization. Other function totals should normally reflect the relative importance of the function. If the chart indicates that more time is being devoted to a function that appears necessary, it must be determined WHY this time is being used. If a function or task involves a complex sequence of steps, a more detailed study should be made. Circle the man-hour totals which seem unreasonable.

(b) Is There Misdirected Effort? Is the organization spending too much time on relatively unimportant or unnecessary work? Instances of misdirected effort are often found in "miscellaneous" or "administrative" categories. The time wasted by any one individual may be small, but it frequently becomes a sizeable total when several individuals are involved. Misdirected effort appears on the Work Distribution Chart when personnel are involved in tasks not contributing directly to the mission of the organization.

(c) Are Skills Being Used Properly? Is everyone being utilized in the best possible manner, or are special skills and abilities being wasted? Personnel of higher grade should not be required to perform tasks which could be performed by lower grade personnel. It is also wasteful to have individuals work out of their field, unless necessary because of varying workloads.

(d) Are Personnel Doing Too Many Unrelated Tasks? A large number of tasks recorded in any one column on a Work Distribution Chart may indicate lost motion and waste of manpower. In studying the chart, it should be remembered that few individuals can perform a variety of tasks equally well.

B-3

Generally, greater manpower efficiency is obtained when an individual performs tasks that have a definite and close relationship with each other. However, overspecialization should not be attempted at the expense of sacrificing organizational flexibility.

(e) Are Tasks Spread Too Thinly? Performance of the same task by more than one individual may indicate duplication of effort. This may cause difficulty in pegging responsibility and further result in procedural and policy inconsistencies, needless interruptions during performance, and loss of time. One person working steadily at a task is usually more productive than several individuals working the same number of man-hours.

(f) Is Work Distributed Evenly? Do total hours indicate that too much work is assigned to one person and not enough to another? From the standpoint of morale one might be as bad as the other. The urgent and important tasks should be spread as evenly as possible to make certain that everyone has a fair day's work and that all work is done according to schedule.

(2) Revision of the Work Distribution Chart. One of the primary purposes of the Work Distribution Chart is to present an overview of the work of the unit and to identify possible areas for improvement. Such things as redistribution of work, change of workflow, space layout, minor organization changes, and other innovations may improve the work situation. Once these proposed changes are checked-out or verified, a new Work Distribution Chart should be produced to reflect the new work distribution picture. This chart may be entitled "recommended organization" and will show the unit's work situation after improvements have been made.

d. Application of the Work Distribution Chart

(1) The purpose of studying and analyzing the work situation and producing a Work Distribution Chart is to help improve the unit's potential to achieve its mission. The chart will assist in achieving the following results:

(a) Elimination of unnecessary tasks.

(b) Reduction of time spent on relatively unimportant functions.

(c) Elimination of duplication and overlapping of work.

(d) Better balance of workloads.

(e) Combination of related tasks.

(f) Realistic estimate of personnel needs.

(g) Better utilization of skills.

(h) Reallocation of misassigned personnel.

(i) Determination of proper allocation of functions to a given organization.

(j) Provision for facilitating the indoctrination of newly assigned personnel.

3. The Flow Process Analysis

    a. Purpose of the Analysis

        (1) A study of work distribution may indicate the need for Flow Process Analysis. The purpose of the analysis is to reduce time and distances involved in a process by eliminating, combining, and changing the sequence of steps in the flow of work.

        (2) The principal tool of this technique is the Flow Process Chart which provides a clear and detailed picture of the flow of work. Recording each step in a procedure helps to identify duplication of effort, back-tracking, and other obstacles to the smooth, efficient flow of work. There are many types of flow process charts. The one considered most applicable to a management survey is the Single-Column Flow Process Chart.

    b. Preparation of Single-Column Flow Process Chart (DD 1723)

        (1) This chart is used to record the steps of a single process. The Single-Column Flow Process Chart (see Tab D) is used to study a single process whether it be a person, paper form or other item.

(a) <u>Heading</u>. In the upper left-hand corner identify the following information: the process to be charted, person or material being charted and the beginning and ending points of the process.

(b) <u>List the Steps</u>. All steps of the process should be listed in brief narrative form in the first column in the sequence in which they occur. This information should be verified with the persons performing the work.

(c) <u>Apply the Symbols</u>. After listing all the steps, the appropriate symbols should be identified for each step. A line should be drawn connecting each symbol. "Distances" are shown when transportations are involved and "quantity" and "time" are shown whenever possible to complete the picture for each step. The individual totals for each type of symbol are entered in the summary box in the upper right-hand corner of the form.

c. <u>Explanation of Symbols</u>

(1) Symbols are used to classify the steps in a process. They assist in the analysis of a process and thereby may point out steps which may be eliminated, combined, rearranged and simplified.

(2) Symbols used in flow process charting are illustrated and explained as follows:

(a) ◯ = Operation - An operation takes place when something is being created, changed, added to, or prepared for another operation, transportation, inspection, or storage. An operation occurs also when information is given or received or when planning or calculating takes place. Examples are:

$\underline{1}$ Typing a letter.
$\underline{2}$ Crating gear.
$\underline{3}$ Repairing a typewriter.
$\underline{4}$ Interviewing a recruit.

(b) ⧐ = Transportation - Transportation occurs when something is moved from one place to another, except when movements are part of an operation or inspection. Examples are:

<u>1</u> A letter is carried to another desk.
<u>2</u> Supplies moved to a commissary.
<u>3</u> A recruit walking to a messhall.

(c)☐ - Inspection - An inspection occurs when an object is examined for identification, quality, quantity or some other characteristic. Examples are:

<u>1</u> Proofreading a letter.
<u>2</u> Verifying weight of supplies for shipment.
<u>3</u> Reviewing pay records for accuracy.

(d) ☐ - Delay - A delay occurs in a process when the flow of an object is interrupted or stopped. Examples are:

<u>1</u> Letter in outgoing box waiting for deliver.
<u>2</u> Waiting in a pay line.
<u>3</u> Holding an item in order to collect a complete shipment.

(e)▽-Storage - Storage occurs when an object is stocked for further use or filed in a cabinet. Examples are:

<u>1</u> Letter in a file cabinet.
<u>2</u> Supplies in a warehouse.

(3) When unusual situations occur which appear to be beyond the definitions offered above, use the following information to determine the proper classification:

Classification	Result
Operation	Produces or accomplishes
Transportation	Movement to another place
Inspection	Examination and verification
Delay	Flow stoppage
Storage	Filed or stocked

d. Analysis of Single-Column Flow Process Chart

(1) The purpose of the flow process chart is to facilitate the detailed and systematic analysis of the process under study. It offers a graphic display of the movement of a man or object through a series of steps necessary to accomplish a job. After all the steps in a process are identified, it becomes relatively easy to study and analyze the process with the purpose of improving it. Improvements can be made by considering the elimination, combination, rearrangement, or simplification of steps and groups of steps in a process. The flow process chart makes it easy to ask the following questions about each step:

(a) WHAT - What is done? What are the steps? What should be done?

(b) WHY - Why is a step done? Why is the process done? Can some steps or the entire process be eliminated?

(c) HOW - How is the work being done? Can it be done in a better manner?

(d) WHO - Who is doing the work? Is he the right person?

(e) WHERE - Where is the process done? Should it be done here? Is it done in the correct sequence? Can the process be combined or simplified? Can the space layout be improved?

(2) As each step is questioned, notes should be made to indicate possible improvements. Types of action to be taken such as eliminating, combining or changing the sequence are checked in the first column of the chart.

e. Application of Single-Column Flow Process Chart

(1) Single-Column Flow Process Charting can be applied to the study and analysis of procedures involving such occasions as:

(a) A major change of personnel, procedures or volume of work.

(b) Making a periodic review of operating methods.

(c) Establishing a new organization.

(d) A procedural problem arises.

THE MANAGEMENT SURVEY

TAB A TO APPENDIX B

TASK LIST

Prepared By G. H. IVERSON	Billet Typist			Grade Cpl.
Supervisor 1stLt. A. B. CANTON	Organization Administrative Division, Maintenance Department			Date 3 Jan 1972
Task Number	Task	Hours Per Week	Work Count	*Posted to Function No.
1.	Type Correspondence	11	25	1
2.	Type Maintenance Requisitions	14	30	4
3.	Type Weekly Maintenance Reports	7	5	5
4.	Prepare Time Reports	10		7
5.	Inventory Office	1		1
	Total Hours Per Week	43		*Completed by Supervisor

TAB B TO APPENDIX B

FUNCTION LIST

Prepared By W. R. CAMPBELL	Title Management Analyst	Grade Major

Organization
   Administrative Division, Maintenance
    Department
		Date
		10 Jan 1972

Function Number	Function	Work Count or Volume (Optional)
1.	Preparation of Correspondence	50
2.	Processing of Incoming Correspondence	220
3.	Maintenance of Central Files	
4.	Administration of Maintenance Funds	
5.	Work Progress Control and Reporting	
6.	Preparation of Maintenance Budget	
7.	Preparation of Time Reports	
8.	Maintenance of Civilian Personnel Records	
9.	Supervision of Division	
10.	Reception of Maintenance Calls and Visitors	
11.	Miscellaneous	

THE MANAGEMENT SURVEY

WORK DISTRIBUTION CHART
TAB C OR APPENDIX B

ORGANIZATIONAL UNIT CHARTED: Administrative Division, Maintenance Department

☑ EXISTING ORGANIZATION ☐ RECOMMENDED ORGANIZATION

CHARTED BY: MAJOR W. R. CAMPBELL

APPROVED BY: _____

DATE: _____

FUNCTION NUMBER	FUNCTION	HOURS PER WEEK	A. B. CANTON — Admin Officer — TASKS	WORK COUNT	HOURS PER WEEK	D. E. FRANKLIN — Stenographer GS-4 — TASKS	WORK COUNT	HOURS PER WEEK	G. H. IVERSON — Typist Cpl — TASKS	WORK COUNT	HOURS PER WEEK	J. K. LATTAMORE — Records Clerk L/Cpl — TASKS	WORK COUNT	HOURS PER WEEK	M. M. OTTINGER — Clerk-Typist L/Cpl — TASKS	WORK COUNT	HOURS PER WEEK	P. Q. RANDOLPH — Receptionist Pfc — TASKS	WORK COUNT	HOURS PER WEEK
1.	Preparation of Correspondence	87	Screen, assign and review correspondence	50	15	Take and Transcribe dictation	50	15	Type Correspondence	20	19	Type correspondence	20	19	Take and transcribe dictation	30	28	Type Correspondence	15	3
2.	Process Incoming Correspondence	15	Screen and route correspondence	220	5											Sort Mail / Maintain Mail Log	220	5 / 5			
3.	Maintenance of Central Files		Supervise Maintenance of files		4	File correspondence		2			2				Maintain Orders & Bulletins Files		3			3
4.	Administrations of Funds	36	Analyze, allocate & report on funds, maintain records of funds		13	Post and Dispatch requisitions	30	13	Type Maintenance requisitions	30	2	Prepare daily labor reports	30	14						
5.	Work Progress Control and Reporting	2	Prepare weekly work report / Maintain "Control & Report" files		11 / 3	Time Weekly Reports		11	Type weekly reports	2	2	Prepare Progress reports / Complete work measurement data	5	4 / 5						
6.	Preparation of Maintenance Budget	2	Prepare Quarterly Budget		2															
7.	Preparation of Time Reports	23	Supervise Timekeeping		1				Prepare time reports			Prepare time distribution cards	10	12						
8.	Maintenance of Civilian Personnel Records	7	Liaison with next higher command		2	Maintain Personnel records	170	5												
9.	Supervision of Division	6	General Supervision																	
10.	Reception of Calls and visitors	13													Receive & route visitors / Answer telephone inquiries / Messenger service	1 / 2	/ 2	Receive & route visitors / Answer telephone inquires	1 / 2	7 / 3
11.	Miscellaneous	17				Collections — Red Cross, etc.		2	Inventory Supplies		4	Sort and distribute savings bonds	20	1				Sort and distribute checks		4
	TOTALS (MAN-HOURS)	247			65			34			43			32			50			23

ANALYSIS: WHAT TAKES THE MOST TIME?...IS THERE MISDIRECTED EFFORT?...ARE SKILLS USED PROPERLY?...ARE THERE TOO MANY UNRELATED TASKS?...ARE TASKS SPREAD TOO THINLY?...IS WORK DISTRIBUTED EVENLY?

DD FORM 1724

B-13

THE MANAGEMENT SURVEY

FLOW PROCESS CHART

TAB D TO APPENDIX B

FLOW PROCESS CHART	NUMBER 1	PAGE NO. 1	NO. OF PAGES 1

PROCESS **Preparation and Distribution of Sick List**
☐ MAN OR ☒ MATERIAL

SUMMARY						
ACTIONS		PRESENT		PROPOSED		DIFFERENCE
		NO.	TIME	NO.	TIME	NO.	TIME
○	OPERATIONS	2	60				
◇	TRANSPORTATIONS	6	—				
☐	INSPECTIONS	4	35				
D	DELAYS	6	80				
▽	STORAGES	—	—				
DISTANCE TRAVELLED (Feet)		504					

CHART BEGINS **List Typed in Admin Office**   CHART ENDS **List delivered to Exec. Officer**

CHARTED BY **Major W. R. CAMPBELL**   DATE **20Jan1971**

ORGANIZATION **Administrative Division, Maintenance Department**

DETAILS OF ☒ PRESENT ☐ PROPOSED   METHOD

#	DETAILS	Operation	Transportation	Inspection	Delay	Storage	Distance in Feet	Quantity	Time	What?	Where?	When?	Who?	How?	NOTES	Eliminate	Combine	Sequence	Place	Person	Improve
1	Sick List typed	○	◇	☐	D	▽			55												
2	List carried to Admin. Chiefs incoming basket	○	◇	☐	D	▽	10														
3	Wait in basket	○	◇	☐	D	▽			5												
4	Proofread by Admin. Chief	○	◇	☐	D	▽			15	x	x	x			Necessary?	x			x		
5	Carried to Admin. Officer's incoming basket	○	◇	☐	D	▽	14														
6	Wait in Basket	○	◇	☐	D	▽			5												
7	Received and initialed by Admin. Officer	○	◇	☐	D	▽	10								Reviewed for accuracy						
8	Carried to Asst. Med. officer's incoming basket	○	◇	☐	D	▽	100									x					
9	Wait in basket	○	◇	☐	D	▽			30							x					
10	Reviewed and initialed by Asst. Med. Officer	○	◇	☐	D	▽			5	x		x			Necessary?	x			x		
11	Wait in outgoing basket	○	◇	☐	D	▽			30							x					
12	Carried to Med. officer's incoming basket	○	◇	☐	D	▽	40														
13	Wait in basket	○	◇	☐	D	▽			5												
14	Reviewed and signed by Med. Officer	○	◇	☐	D	▽			5						Reviewed for information						
15	Wait in outgoing basket	○	◇	☐	D	▽			55												
16	Carried to file clerks desk in Admin. Office	○	◇	☐	D	▽	140								By Messenger						
17	Copies sorted for distribution	○	◇	☐	D	▽			5												
18	Original carried to executive officer	○	◇	☐	D	▽	200														
19		○	◇	☐	D	▽															
20		○	◇	☐	D	▽															
21		○	◇	☐	D	▽															

THE MANAGEMENT SURVEY

APPENDIX C

ANALYSIS CHECKLIST

1. Programs and Policies

a. What are the principal programs and policies of the organization?

b. What does each program and policy contribute to the mission of the organization? What would be the consequence if any were discontinued?

c. Are programs and policies being actively accomplished?

d. Is there any unnecessary duplication or overlapping in any program?

e. Are programs and policies coordinated and kept current?

f. Are programs and policies clearly and concisely defined in writing?

g. Are all personnel concerned kept informed of the initiation of new programs and policies and changes to existing ones?

2. Organization and Functions

a. Does the activity have an organization manual showing its organization structure, mission, and functions and those of its subordinate units? Is the manual accurate? Is the manual kept current?

b. Is the organization structure and the assignment of functions logical to best accomplish the programs and carry out the policies? Are there too many or too few organization layers? Is there evidence of "empire-building"?

c. Is the span of control reasonable?

d. Are the functions assigned to each unit and the tasks assigned to each person specific, clear-cut, and similar?

e. Are responsibility and authority delegated to the lowest level where the work can be accomplished? Is there overlapping or conflicting delegation?

THE MANAGEMENT SURVEY

f. Is authority to direct an individual limited to one person? Does each person know to whom he reports?

g. Does management exercise control through attention to policy problems and assign review of routine actions of subordinates to lower echelons?

h. Are staff units available to provide assistance as required in specialized areas? Do they violate channels of command?

3. Procedures

a. Are all procedures covered by written instructions?

b. Have the steps in each major procedure been analyzed? Can any of the operations be eliminated of combined with others? Can the procedure be simplified or improved by changing the sequence of operations?

c. Have standardized procedures been adopted wherever feasible?

d. Should any procedure, being performed manually, be automated?

e. How often are procedures reviewed with an aim toward improvement?

f. Do personnel who are responsible for carrying out procedures participate in developing necessary changes?

4. Personnel Requirements and Workload

a. Is workload used to determine staffing?

b. Is staffing based on a formal system of evaluating performance?

c. Have steps been taken to analyze workload, determine whether it is increasing or decreasing, and to eliminate the causes for backlogs?

d. What can be done to eliminate large variations in the volume of workload to obtain an even flow?

e. Are plans made to meet predictable increases and decreases of workloads?

f. Do the most important functions receive the most time? Is too much time spent on relatively unimportant or unnecessary work?

g. What can be done to eliminate or reduce overtime?

h. Is "make-ready" time kept to a necessary minimum?

i. Have controls been established to assure that the important projects and the oldest work receive priority attention?

5. Manpower Utilization

a. Are employee skills being properly used? Is each individual doing the work he is best qualified for?

b. What are the causes of absenteeism and turnover? What can be done to correct them?

c. Does each person understand his job? Has he been furnished with a copy of his job description, if one has been prepared?

d. Is job enrichment practiced on hard-to-fill positions wherever practicable?

e. Are employees used in other operations during slack periods in their regular work?

f. Work assignments:

(1) Is work distributed unevenly -- too much work for one employee and not enough for another?

(2) Is work spread too thinly -- is there needless interruption, inconsistency, and buck-passing because too many persons are doing the same thing?

(3) Are employees doing too many unrelated assignments, making it impossible to evaluate effectiveness?

g. Do supervisory-employee relations contribute to activity effectiveness? If not, what can be done to improve them?

h. Does employee morale or employee discipline present a problem? How can they be improved?

6. Quality and Quantity of Work

a. What reviews or inspections are used to insure acceptable quality? Are they effective? Are there too many or too few?

b. Have realistic quantity standards been set? Are they being met?

c. Are the reviews worth the cost in terms of frequency and significance of errors?

d. Is the quality standard higher than the use justifies?

e. What causes the errors? Can errors be reduced at the source?

f. Are pen corrections made when practicable to avoid retyping work?.

g. Could spot checks replace detailed reviews?

h. Would clarification of procedures or instructions reduce errors?

7. Records Management

a. Forms Management

(1) Are the services of the local forms management personnel used to review and control forms for simplification, or discontinuance?

(2) Are forms design and control manuals used?

(3) Are any forms used which have not been standardized? If so, why?

b. Reports Management

(1) What reports are received by the organization? For what purpose?

(2) What reports are prepared by the organization? For what purpose?

(3) Do either required or prepared reports contain information which duplicates that already conveniently available from other sources?

(4) Can any reporting requirements be eliminated or reduced without impairing the operations of the activity?

(5) Are reporting requirements reviewed periodically? How long has it been since the last review was made of every report? Were any reports eliminated, combined, or revised?

(6) Are all locally-required reports controlled?

(7) Would further delegation of authority eliminate any reports?

c. Documentation Management

(1) Do records disposal schedules cover all records?

(2) Are records disposal schedules being applied?

8. Office Equipment

a. What types and quantities of office machines are in use?

b. Is each piece of office equipment appropriate for the job? Is it properly maintained in good operating condition?

c. Is equipment located for most extensive use? Should there be more sharing of equipment?

d. Should any equipment be released for more effective use elsewhere?

e. Should a machine be used to replace manual methods?

f. Are the machines used sufficiently to justify their cost?

9. Office Layout

a. Does the arrangement of furniture and equipment provide for the most effective utilization of space?

b. Are desks and equipment arranged to permit a straight-line flow of work?

c. Are units and personnel having a great deal of in-and-out traffic situated near entrances?

d. Is the space properly lighted, heated and ventilated?

e. Are related work units situated near each other?

f. Does the office layout facilitate effective supervision?

g. Does the office layout provide for the maintenance of necessary security precautions?

10. Correspondence Management

a. Are pattern paragraphs and letters used whenever practicable instead of dictation or manually-prepared rough drafts?

b. Are preprinted form letters used whenever practicable?

c. Do the typists use correspondence shortcuts?

THE MANAGEMENT SURVEY

APPENDIX D

COMMON MISTAKES MADE BY ANALYSTS

1. Pitfalls caused by inadequate preparations for surveys:

a. Failure to define clearly the mission of the survey.

b. Failure to have a clear-cut understanding with top management regarding the survey, its purposes, and the action to be taken on the findings.

c. Failure to establish proper relationships between the survey staff and the organization being surveyed.

d. Failure to put definite boundaries around the survey; that is, a failure to limit properly the scope.

2. Failures due to poor fact gathering:

a. Failure to study background material such as previous surveys, budget documents, outside criticisms, etc., before attempting to gather facts regarding current operations.

b. Use of superficial fact-gathering techniques when only first hand observation, testing, etc., will give accurate information upon which action can be based.

c. Failure to keep accurate and complete records of the facts gathered, properly arranged so that they can be intelligently studied in later phases of the survey.

3. Failures caused by inadequate or incorrect analysis of data:

a. Failure to discuss facts with the organization being surveyed or with others in a position to know in order to determine whether or not the data really means what it seems to mean.

b. Failure to check the facts learned from one source with facts learned from other sources in order to be sure that they are properly integrated.

c. Common tendency to jump to conclusions and to use pattern solutions.

d.   Tendency to form early prejudices and to attempt to make later findings support these prejudices.

e.   Failure to use the best tools for integrating and interpreting facts.

f.   Tendency to spend too much time on the analysis, thus making the data upon which recommendations must be based so out of date that management does not have full confidence that they represent current situations.

4.   <u>Failures caused by faulty reporting of survey results</u>:

(1) Failure to discuss survey recommendations with people who will have to live with them, particularly the management of the organization surveyed.

b.   Failure to convince these people of the benefits to be derived from the recommendations.

c.   Tendency to deal in personalities instead of with objective material.

d.   Tendency of some analysts to put their own personalities into reports; to claim credit which does not belong to them; to claim credit which does belong to them but which might better be unmentioned.

e.   Failure to summarize properly and to organize the net results of the survey in brief form so that management can take action without too much digging into detail.

f.   Failure to use visual aids to explain the more complicated principles involved.

g.   Failure to consider properly the personalities involved; sometimes better results are obtained when no report at all is submitted and the whole matter is handled orally.

5.   <u>Failures caused by inadequate follow-up</u>:

a.   The common tendency and feeling that the administrative analysis staff should only make recommendations and that it should be completely divorced from installation responsibilities.

b. Tendency to concentrate survey effort on current problems with the result that completed projects are not adequately checked to see that the recommendations are actually in effect in their intended form and are accomplishing their intended purposes.

c. In some instances, the administrative analysis staff errs in the opposite direction by completely installing its recommendations, leaving the management of the organization surveyed out of the picture and completely unprepared to maintain and support the changes made.